A speck of dust

Parveen Choudhury

A speck of dust © 2024 Parveen Choudhury

All rights reserved.

No part of this publication may be reproduced, stored in a retrieval system, or transmitted, in any form or by any means, electronic, mechanical, photocopying, recording or otherwise, without the prior written permission of the presenters.

Parveen Choudhury asserts the moral right to be identified as author of this work.

Presentation by *BookLeaf Publishing*

Web: www.bookleafpub.com

E-mail: info@bookleafpub.com

ISBN:9789358310580

First edition 2024

DEDICATION

to my speck of dust Sadiq, and my nature incarnations Ocean and Earth. also to my mother who gave me this wonderful life and is still protecting me, and my father who made me who i am.

ACKNOWLEDGEMENT

The poems appear in chronological time. From a depressed teenager saved by love to a woman ravaged by the trials of motherhood saved by nature, the written word has been a feeble attempt to find solace and connection in this journey.

Please note that I have used 'i' instead of 'I' throughout my poems intentionally. This is not a typo or error. I used the small letter 'i' in my poems to express my inner self authentically and stay away from the ego that 'I' represents in the world.

PREFACE

The musician performs on the stage for an audience what a writer performs on the page for a reader.

The musician practices to perform to an audience, what the musician offers is a performance in time. The listener enjoys the artist in the present, in the moment.

The writer performs mostly solitary and mostly to himself, what the writer offers is a practice through time. The reader listens to the artist across time and space. What is on offer is a capsule of time travel.

Table of Contents

a mother still living inside you

how does a mother live in you long after she is
gone.
through her rituals, her routines, and her prayers.
through her shortcomings, her failings, her
regrets.
through her stories, of her own mother, or lack
thereof
through her hopes, her songs,
through her old jewelry she was saving for your
wedding
through her old sarees she wished you would
inherit
through memories of her freshly washed hair
and milk scented skin
through memories of her banging her head on
the wall in rage
and beating you up
through her will to do better tomorrow, and by
you
through her hopes to do better with you
through her hopes to be a better mother than her
mother

all her hopes which are now yours.

2

sangeeta- my soft music

Until yesterday life was bleak, smile was sleek
Tomorrow onwards, it would be the same trick
It is today that is joy, mirth
For you haunt my senses, my sweetheart
You bloomed my life like no one else
Captured the pearl from the hardest of shells
Now I ponder what you have done
Stolen the burning rage of the sun
You will leave kissed dews on my life's petal
And your memories will torment like the
Hard clink on my heart turned to cold metal

let me in

when you urged, "let me in"
into the long night,
it was not just my womb
i was opening upto you,
it was my very soul
i was letting you into.

when we think
time heals everything,
we forget
time steals everything.

first plants

I water myself daily so I can grow.
Just like I tend to my plants,
Pruning dead leaves,
Checking the soil,
Maybe the rubber needs some more sunshine
Maybe the pathos is overwatered

I prune my stems so I can grow
Snipping feeble habits
So I can grow bushier in that what serves me

I unfurl my leaves in the sweet sunshine of the
morning
And await for abundant flowering
Hoping that some of those
Shall seed into that which is beyond my wild
imaginings

I fertilise the soil of my mind and body
I write, paint, run, read, and breathe
I become a willing part of the cycle of nature

I remind myself that balance is the way of
growth
A sheltered plant often dies when overwatered

Maybe you forgot to put a hole in the bottom of
the pot
Now how do they let go of yesterday's shit?

for a palm sized son

into the endless night
my womb emptied out
my little boy i named Meer
now buried in the rocks of the Dharwar craton
butterflies guarding earthworms wriggling
he became one with the earth

my tired feet
scorching through the desert
kept running
and i chanced on a stone so clear
like a universe of light
i picked it and held it to my heart
i ran and more stones called out
clear quartz like ice
moss agate like forest stream
citrine like sunshine
tourmaline like the black night

bloodstone like living flesh
amethyst like sweet luck
I melted into them
healed and held by these healer friends

we look for the black holes and galaxies beyond
but what if we could make a full circle
and find them right here in these crystals
a mote of dust in the stars
a star in these motes of dust

my son has become a crystal in some universe
and maybe a lost mother finds him someday
maybe I have found him already
attaining nirvana, peaceful in a stone of light.

a god sings

first rain
drenching me
barefoot
dancing on the road
hot soft mud
smelling a long forgotten life

awakening sleeping seeds
calling for all to rise
the flurry of activity
the fury of thunder
the feisty rain

even the wooden chairs dance
and drape in moss green

seeds growing in boots
tiles cracks holes ears
drumming humming hears
god in action

for it is god who sings and
dances and shows in the
monsoon

music that finds you

soft is the music
that catches you unaware

old Bollywood songs
blasting on a street shop
Himesh Reshammiya
still surooring at a butcher's

carnatic raga
from within fluttering curtains
the song of old stones in Hampi

a mother's lost lullaby in a dream

a bird chirping
drowning your sobs
a baby's laughter in a running train

pitter patter of rain on a bus window
a seeker singing sufi bhakti
in a dusty town

tea boiling during an argument
love making in a hotel room

urine susurrating on dry earth
Crickets stars
owl hooting on a dark night

a loved one's breath after a nightmare
like some soft melody sneaking in a falling
house

finding my breath

when rage took over I thrashed
glass utensils mirror bottles ukulele
I beat myself I cut myself
my cats my baby my love all were scared

when misery took over I ran
other places people things spaces
I left myself
my home bereft

when sadness took over I cried
helpless lonely scared abandoned
I wanted to kill
myself my love myself my family

when I heard divine music I breathed
a sigh peace rest love safety

I became love myself my love myself my
universe

when   my breathe   took over   I found
home   in myself   meaning   in   self

my boobs

when they first sprouted
like buds on my chest
aunties teased that
the daughter is ripening
"be careful to cover her"
I kept collecting mangoes
pretending unawareness
but a little hunched now
to cover my shameful buds

when they began to blossom
like flowers on my chest
my mother teased me
that they were getting much too bigger
she got padded bra to flatten them
which only made them stouter
while I hunched even more
to hide my communal shame

when they glowed
like diamonds on my chest
my boyfriends held them in awe
drinking deep from their nectar
cradling their faces between them
I felt love for them

I hunched a bit less
my girlfriends advised miracle bras and cotton
bras
to once again hide my shame

when they fruited
like jackfruits on my body
my babies suckled from them deep
sweet white sap overflowed
they clung to them like roots to the ground
sleeping on their billowy folds
I rooted a feet deep and became Mother Earth

but now they were much too unconventional for
the society
renegades defying bras
overhanging contentedly on my belly
I longed for the perkiness of yesterday,
mourning the women who had continued the
shame
that befell their bodies
I cried, my boobs heaved
we both drenched in the rain of feminine sorrow

until I looked up and saw a mango tree
laden with luscious fruit
a pair of them shining golden
just like my two sweet breasts

and I became a mango tree
proud and tall and bountiful
my mangoes the greatest treasure
I reaped in this life

their miraculous milk
food for my seeds
their smooth texture
a beckoning to my lover
now I dance in the moonlight
uninhibited
my twin stars finally free and shining for all to
see

self care

is it self care
when you cage your body in wired bras,
slap lipstick,
slather potions,
and pout
for the world to see
and buy some more.
it is self expectation.

when you desire to be admired
by the millions
yet your skin screams
and pores weep
when every look at the mirror
is filled with trepidation
every time your body feels short of social
expectation

it is self care
when you finally let your breasts hang free
and lie on the soft green grass
daring to bare your skin to the sun
do you dare to ignore all that sunscreen advice

when the rains dance on you

and wind paints your face softly
in shades of earthy tones and joy
foraged flowers adorning your hair
crushed petals on your lips
the body suffused with moss and rain

when you know when to eat
and when to stop
sing under the trees
dance in the sea
one in all, all in one
looking at the mirror
you can say hi, hello there, i love you,
you unique piece of life and adventure

when you touch your skin and caress all of it
splash water to nurture it
when after a lifetime of being used by the
economy
you finally refuse to let others make money out
of your body
finally you can hug your body
and ask
what is it you need today my love

this is self care, this is self love
beyond the fields of cosmetics and commercials
there is a field,
you will meet your self love there

a life named Ocean

i went to the shore carrying my bleeding womb
i took a walk with the waves
day after day i walked
and i still bled with the moon
i felt the sand cave beneath my feet
and prayed to the sea

it gave me a gift-
a beautiful shell

i picked it up
and another, and another
the rocks arose and dipped
the rains came and went
my room filled up with
Seashells.
and slowly i made a
Beautiful bed of dead things
to lie with my mate

as the sun set like a melon one day,
i found a moon snail so perfect
and he found another moon snail so perfect
we exclaimed that they fit and marvelled
and i prayed to the sea again

to gift me a life
and i will name it Ocean

and thus Ocean was born
a blessing from the sea

a life named Earth

by the river Ganga i sat to meditate
my womb still sore, my breasts spent
my nights awake and my soul sapped

as my guru spoke softly, i slept
a sleep of million years, a silence night deep
by the river Ganga, i flowed
i stepped on her womb
and i found her sparkling seeds
rocks so old, pebbles like patterned gold

stones that were tombs for ammonites
stones that sang of ice ages
stones as old as time

i picked them up and sang with them
Ganga had gifted me stones to take back to my
Ocean
or so i thought

but also to connect me deeper with my mother
mother Ganga had sprouted in my womb
a seed so precious
a seed of her spirit
that i named Earth

the universe/multiverse

you say i have to learn the language of the boss
that He only speaks THE language
verses of which he sent from the sky
to HIS chosen man

you tie my head in a scarf
start young, you say
to men who smell of sweet perfume
kohl lined eyes, drinking sweet tea,
no, not cough, its Qaf!

when i ask what does it all anyway mean
you call me a kafir
when i ask how do you know what a baby is?
they all look the same to me
same blood, same cry, same innocence
you call me friends of kafir
when i ask how can reciting a verse while dying
confirm a slot for me in heaven
what about being good
and what about my dear friend the kafir

do they simply burn in eternity
they were anyway allotted to gods by chance
you call me the spawn of the devil

i go to school
and chant gayatri mantra
but you won't sit near me
you will whisper to each other
she eats 'that'
'that' that is unspeakable
'that' that changes for every God
'that' that i have eaten for all of you
and still feel holy
may all 'that' nourished me rest in peace

i can go on and on
but let me rest peacefully too

i grew up weary and lonely
with a God-shaped hole in my heart
parents hurt, lovers went,
and you all kept me away from God

i sat in temples swaying to chants
i sat in the church singing hymns,
i kept away from the ones by birth,
for i anyway never belonged to them

do the plants know the language of the boss

do the birds sing in HIS language too
does the vast ocean carry tides in his chants

when i saw i was part of nature-
they are not just animals,
oceans land sky not just resources for His
favourite creation
you are only a mere few thousand old entrant
in a billion-year-old drama of life
if those in known time and beyond
can talk to HIM and pray in their language

and wait!
i don't even think it's a Him even
when did you ever hear of a Him
giving birth to anything
I know it's a Her
but for God's sake let's stop
with this him/her/they/them/anyone

i call this thing we are all afraid of
and pray to and want to appease
and appeal
and most suddenly fervently
start believing in
when we are sick, dying,
have become new parents,
are in debt, or just want help from
THE UNIVERSE

the universe/multiverse (let's be inclusive even
here)
likes to be appreciated, sung to, serenaded,
after all, as I said, it is feminine

i went to the beach and found her
the sky aglow, the sand soft,
even the dead showing the miracle in their
shells,
the waves Her language of love
i looked and prayed to her
told her how beautiful all that she created was
may all her creations, beautiful, large, and small
continue to exist
may fire as it destroys
continue to create new fertile land for her babies
may all that give birth be protected
and their children flourish
may life animate, innate, elemental always
flourish
she was water
that gave life on earth
i prayed to her
that even when the sun has stopped burning
may her creations find its way to new planets
and galaxies

though i know i will depart of this consciousness
soon someday
may i always feel her presence and sing her
praises in wonder
and the purest love
in all other forms of consciousness that i take

i think She liked all i said and prayed,
for i have been quite happy and peaceful since
i feel protected by her
she had always been beside and within me

the hole in my heart has now become a galaxy
full of
love and wonder, praise be to my universe.

www.ingramcontent.com/pod-product-compliance
Lightning Source LLC
La Vergne TN
LVHW021301200726

843509LV00012B/1734